Fitness, Fun and Friends
Stories from a remarkable life

by Linda A. LeVasseur

KDP Publishing

Copyright 2020

Linda LeVasseur Walkins

ISBN: 978-0-9856951-3-2

Dedicated to Gerald B. LeVasseur and Marion Blanchard LeVasseur

Acknowledgements

Writing this memoir for my father, Jerry LeVasseur, has been a rewarding endeavor. I have learned about his countless achievements, his strength, his unique view on life, and the amazing impact he has had on so many people.

Thank you to everyone who has contributed "Jerry Stories" to this narrative: Charlie Berdahl, Bill Borla, Dick Burns, Holly Lyne, Julia O'Rourke, Dr. Herbert Paris, Lara-Jane Que, Peter Slovenski, Bridger Tomlin, Ben Torda.

Additionally, I must thank my sister, Karen LeVasseur, for her excellent editorial critique of the manuscript. She has helped shape this book about our father. With her insights, I hope you will get to know the real Jerry LeVasseur as you read his life stories.

Most importantly, many thanks to you, Dad, for asking me to write this book for you. Like you, I hope your story will help others who have faced adversity and inspire young athletes to always "run through the finish line."

Table of Contents

Preface

"My grandfather is an incredible man. I've never met anyone with the passion or dedication that he has." —Justin Franco

Last summer, my parents Jerry and Arden LeVasseur, traveled to Albuquerque, New Mexico to participate in the National Senior Games. During the week, Jerry was featured in an article published in the *Albuquerque Journal* in which he recounted how he has overcome personal tragedy through positivity and determination. As he told the news reporter, he is always looking ahead to what's next. Jerry's indomitable spirit has sustained him throughout his remarkable life.

Jerry and Arden are both Senior Games. enthusiasts.
They last competed in New Mexico.

Born on November 19, 1937, Jerry is the son of Ludger Wilfred LeVasseur and Marion Blanchard LeVasseur. The young family lived in Bristol, Connecticut just outside the state capital, Hartford. Ludger ran a grocery store, First National, in the town's French neighborhood and Marion worked as a registered nurse at Bristol Hospital. Jerry has fond memories of his early childhood. He speaks nostalgically of his black dog, Halley, playing baseball, skiing on a nearby hilly field, and fishing in the stream that ran behind his house.

Those carefree days ended abruptly on July 6, 1944. Six-year-old Jerry, his mother, Marion, and some friends were headed to the Ringling Bros. and Barnum & Bailey circus. It was a scorching hot day and while standing at the bus stop, they wondered if they should postpone their circus trip. However, the bus to Hartford arrived and the group climbed aboard.

Young Jerry in Bristol

At 2:40 pm, as the wild lion act concluded, the circus tent caught fire. Marion did her utmost to protect Jerry from the flames and lost her life. Jerry was pulled from the burning tent and spent the next five months recuperating in the hospital. He suffered burns on his hands, back, and head. Jerry did not learn of his mother's death until several weeks later. His father, who had wanted to keep the news from Jerry while he was in such critical condition, finally told Jerry of his mother's passing during a hospital visit. At age 11, Jerry would undergo the first of three operations to give him more functionality in his hands, which had been severely burned. He was fortunate to be under the care of a skilled plastic surgeon at Presbyterian Hospital in New York, who repaired his hands so that Jerry could develop a stronger grip and grasp items with more dexterity.

When Jerry returned home and went back to school, he had to contend with bullying. Classmates taunted him because of the bald patch on his head and the deformity of his hands. Jerry got into fights, but he did not let the mean-spirited acts of his classmates keep him down. Instead, Jerry was determined to prove the bullies wrong. He was a kid just like them and he knew he could still participate in all the regular boyhood activities.

Fortunately, Jerry was sustained by his faith in God and by the love and attention of his maternal grandmother. Luella Violet Blanchard (née Sherman) otherwise known as Nana Laurie spent a lot of time with her grandson as he was growing up.

Additionally, Nana Laurie had a family friend named Tom Rocray, who became a mentor and a role model for young Jerry.

Jerry and his grandmother

Jerry attended high school at the prep school, The Gunnery, in Washington, Connecticut. As required, he was active in school sports. In his senior year, he was named captain of the school's Third Basketball and Third Football teams. He also served on the Student Council.

On January 8, 1956, during his senior year at the prep school, Jerry attended an ice skating party in Milford hosted by a local church. At the party, he met Arden Crocker, who had been invited to the party by a family friend, Barbara Brotherton. Jerry wrote to Arden after the party and they had their first date in New Haven. They met on the street corner near Jerry's orthodontist office and then went to the movies to see "Picnic" starring William Holden and Kim Novak.

Jerry and Arden dated during their remaining high school years and while Arden was at nursing school in Stamford. They often spent time in New York City, both taking the train in and meeting under the clock at the

Biltmore Hotel. While in the city, they enjoyed frequenting jazz clubs and once saw Dave Brubeck perform.

Upon his graduation from The Gunnery in 1956, Jerry looked forward to the next chapter in his life at Lehigh University. At Lehigh, Jerry forged friendships with his fraternity brothers in Sigma Phi. He was also involved in the Brown Key Society, the Newman Club and the Ski Club. After transferring from the school of engineering to become an accounting major, Jerry studied diligently to prepare himself for his career as a certified public accountant. For the majority of his career, Jerry worked as the Chief Financial Officer of Pratt-Read, a mid-sized manufacturing company in Connecticut.

On September 17, 1960, Jerry and Arden were married at the St. Mary Catholic Church in Branford, CT. They celebrated with their family and friends at the Owenego Beach Club. After honeymooning in the Poconos, the couple moved into an apartment in Bethlehem, PA. Jerry completed a final semester at Lehigh and went on to take additional accounting courses after graduation.

Jerry and Arden on their wedding day.

Eventually, the newlyweds settled on the Connecticut shoreline and raised four daughters in the towns of North Branford and Madison. Jerry joined the civic organization, the United States Junior Chamber (Jaycees) and took an active part in community projects in both Connecticut towns.

Always a proponent of physical fitness, Jerry enjoyed a variety of athletic pursuits while he and Arden raised their family. Jerry was a loyal member of a local softball team sponsored by Franco's Package Store. He and Arden purchased land and built a ski chalet in Wilmington, VT. The family took many weekend skiing trips. Jerry also took up jogging, eventually becoming a daunting competitor in Masters and Senior races around the world. Additionally, Jerry enjoyed a successful career as a dogsled driver.

Jerry and Arden have been married for nearly 60 years. Throughout their life together, they have traveled the globe. In the early years, they traveled to accounting conventions, visiting countries like Mexico and Spain. Later, Arden began to sing in her church choirs and a group called Capella Cantorum. Jerry accompanied her and her fellow singers on many European tours. The group explored many countries including England, Portugal and Belgium while singing in famous cathedrals. Jerry and Arden have continued their travels to compete in the World Senior Games, going as far as New Zealand to race.

In his journeys, with his camera in hand, Jerry has become an accomplished photographer. His Flickr account contains nearly 200,000 photographs from all over the world. On one of his most memorable trips to Botswana and South Africa, Jerry took many stunning wildlife photographs.

Jerry and Arden traveled to Africa in 2012.

In 2015, Jerry entered a photo contest sponsored by Vantage Travel. He submitted several photos and his family, friends and the student athletes he coached at Bowdoin College showed their support by casting votes for Jerry's photos. His picture of a young girl on the streets of Istanbul won the grand prize—a free river cruise in France.

Jerry and Arden retired to Brunswick, Maine in 2004. Wanting to give back, Jerry contacted the athletics department at Bowdoin College, offering his service as a volunteer coach. To this day, he works with the young athletes on the Cross Country and Track teams, teaching them that they can do whatever they want if they put their mind to it.

Every spring, Jerry and Arden host a cook-out for the graduating athletes at their home in Brunswick. The annual get-together has become a much-appreciated tradition.

The 75th Anniversary of the Circus Fire was observed on July 6, 2019 at the Hartford Circus Fire Memorial on Barbour Street, which had been created in 2005. Jerry and Arden attended the memorial service and Jerry was featured in an article published in *The Hartford Courant* that week.

In the article, Jerry explained why he viewed the horrific experience as an opportunity to overcome adversity and become stronger. Although he suffered sorrow and pain because of the fire, Jerry faced those difficulties head on and worked hard to keep them from overshadowing his life.

Hartford Circus Fire Memorial (photos courtesy of L. Walkins)

Since the anniversary, Jerry has received phone calls and letters from other survivors and their family members. In turn, he has reached out to those who contacted him to share his positive philosophy. He hopes talking about his experiences has been helpful to others scarred by the fire.

In addition to approaching life with determination and positivity, Jerry also gives 100% to any athletic contest, activity or hobby he takes on. He has received much deserved recognition and countless medals and awards for his efforts in dogsled racing and competitive running. Jerry has been featured in many media articles and friends and fellow runners have suggested he should write a book about his life experiences. Jerry hopes this collection of stories will help others who have faced or are facing adversity in their lives.

Today, Jerry still looks to the future with hope and optimism. So, what's next? Undoubtedly, Jerry will continue to create and gather photos, memories and new life stories to add to this collection.

Linda A. LeVasseur
Quincy, MA

ᵾ ᵾ ᵾ

July 6, 1944

"She saved my life." —Jerry

S tanding on the corner near his father's grocery store, First National in Bristol's French neighborhood, Jerry held his mother Marion's hand. Their neighbors, Mrs. Eustice and the Linxweilers were there too. They were waiting for the bus to Hartford because the Ringling Bros. Barnum & Bailey circus was in town. All of the kids on Burlington Street were excited about the circus. Today, Jerry was going to see the wild animals, the clowns and all of the other circus performers.

Jerry and his parents and grandmother in his backyard in Bristol, CT.

Jerry squinted up at the blazing July sun and listened to the grown-ups talk about the extremely hot weather.

"Maybe we shouldn't go," someone said.

Jerry exchanged a glance with Mrs. Linxweiler's daughter, MaryAnn. Were they going to have to miss the circus? But then while the grown-ups were still talking, the bus rumbled down the street and pulled to a stop in front of them.

The bus doors opened with a whoosh and they all climbed aboard. Jerry sat by an open window with his mother beside him. A warm breeze ruffled his hair as the bus rolled toward the city. Watching the houses, trees and cars flash by the window, he grinned to himself and wondered if he would get to see lions and elephants at the circus.

An air of excitement lit up the crowded circus grounds. Hundreds of people happily swarmed toward the big tent. After paying for their tickets, Marion and Jerry climbed up into the stands and took their seats. Jerry could see everything that was going on in the three rings below. Some men were moving animal cages around, getting ready for the first act.

At last, the ringmaster started the show. Jerry watched intently as the animal trainers had the elephants and big cats show off the tricks they had learned. He thought being an animal trainer when he grew up might be fun.

The trapeze act was next. The famous flying Wallenda family was waiting high above them, ready to perform. Suddenly, the circus band began to play the song "Stars and Stripes Forever" and the Wallendas climbed down from the trapeze platform.

Everyone around Jerry was asking what was going on. In the far right corner of the tent flames burned high up against the ceiling.

Jerry looked at his mother in confusion as they stood up and climbed down from the stands along with their neighbors and the rest of the audience. Smoke started to fill the big top.

They rushed toward the spot where they had walked into the tent. The large animal cages blocked the entrance. The crowd pushed forward to a group of policemen who were helping people climb up over the cages to safety. Everyone looked frightened.

A policeman held out his hand to Jerry and his mother. In just a few moments they would escape from the hot and smoky tent. As they reached up toward the policeman, someone pushed them from behind and Jerry and Marion fell to the ground.

Lying beneath his mother, who was trying to protect him, Jerry listened to people screaming all around him. Soon he lost track of time. The next thing he knew, a man wearing a white shirt was carrying him outside. Jerry was glad to be out of the heat and the confusion of the tent. But where was his mother?

Someone put Jerry into a taxi along with a bunch of ladies and their kids. Even though Jerry sat by himself in the corner of the cab, he didn't cry like all of the other children. The driver drove as fast as he could to the closest hospital.

At the hospital, Jerry lay on a bed inside an oxygen tent. The oxygen was helping him breathe. He could hear the nurses and doctors walking by and talking.

"Who's in this oxygen tent?" someone asked.

"A little boy. His injuries are quite serious. I don't think he's going to make it," another voice replied.

Jerry knew they were talking about him. *Oh yes, I will,* he thought to himself.

And despite the odds, he did.

ᶾ ᶾ ᶾ

NOTE: The story of July 6, 1944 is presented through young Jerry's point of view. The events described are based on his memories of that day. In order to present a full picture of what happened that day, the following background information will illuminate how miraculous it was that Jerry survived.

In the chaos and confusion of the spectators' mass exit from the burning tent, Jerry and his mother, Marion, were trapped in a mob of people in the area of the northeast chute. The exit was blocked and the crowd was out of control. When Marion was knocked down, she lay on top of Jerry to protect him from the fire and the trampling feet. They ended up buried in a pile of charred bodies. Only Jerry and four or five other people were still alive. The police officers, who had reached for Marion's hand, were still on duty. They helped carry out the bodies piled up at the northeast chute.

The scenes outside the burning tent and at the hospital were just as chaotic. Parents searched frantically for their lost children. Those children wandered alone not knowing what to do or where to go.

Most of the casualties ended up at Municipal Hospital, which was just a few blocks from the circus grounds. The hard-working medical staff was soon overwhelmed. Jerry was placed in an oxygen tent. He had burns over 25% of his body. Loose skin hung from his arms. He was missing fingers on both hands. Eventually, Jerry was moved from the oxygen tent and placed in a bed beside another injured boy. Jerry wished he had a pillow like the other boy, but there were none to be had.

That night, when relative quiet had settled over the hospital, those in charge decided to transfer some patients to either Hartford Hospital or St. Francis Hospital to alleviate the overcrowding at Municipal. Jerry was sent to Hartford Hospital.

Meanwhile, Jerry's father was trying to locate his wife and son. He made the rounds of the three hospitals and a local school, where many of the lost children were waiting for their parents to claim them. Finally, Ludger found Jerry at the hospital, severely injured but clinging to life.

The dead had been taken to the armory building in Hartford. A total of 167 people died as a result of the fire. The corpses, some burnt beyond recognition, were laid out on army cots.

Marion LeVasseur is interred at St. Joseph's Cemetery.

On July 7, the day after the fire, Ludger identified Marion's body and then headed to Providence, RI to break the horrible news to her family. He would wait several weeks before telling Jerry that his mother had passed away. Marion was buried at St. Joseph's Cemetery in Bristol, CT (O'Nan).

❊ ❊ ❊

Dogs, Dogs, Dogs

"Some people had pools, some had grass, we had dogs." — Jerry

Charles Schultz and his Peanuts gang insisted that, "Happiness is a warm puppy." Jerry LeVasseur could not agree more. From a young age, dogs have had an indelible impact on Jerry's life. As he was growing up, he enjoyed the companionship of the family pet, Halley, a shaggy black dog and later on his grandmother, Nana Laurie's boxer, Bootsie.

Jerry, Marion and Halley

When Jerry and Arden married, they welcomed a perky Scottish terrier into the family, naming her Lass. Lass grew up alongside the LeVasseur daughters first on Twin Lakes Road in North Branford and then on Princess Drive in Madison. She was a loyal member of the family. Although she passed away long ago at the age of 14 (72 in human years), Lass has been immortalized in family movies. In the old films, the playful terrier eternally romps with her "sisters" in the front yard in Madison.

Arden, her mother Fran and Lass in front of 47 Twin Lakes Road.

When Lass got older and started to slow down, the LeVasseurs decided to get another dog. Jerry was interested in adopting a puppy from a litter of Siberian Huskies raised by a friend on his softball team. His next-door neighbor, Joe Fitzgerald, who was also on the team, and Jerry each took home a puppy. The two canine sisters, Nina and Natasha, settled into life on Princess Drive.

Nina

Intrigued by the up and coming sport of sled dog racing, Jerry did some research about the breed. Eagerly, he joined a new local Siberian club and went to his first race as a spectator. He thoroughly enjoyed the experience and was inspired to take on the challenge of learning a new sport.

When Jerry acquired two additional Siberians, Nikki and Princess, he purchased the necessary equipment, including a sled, harnesses, lines and a three-wheeled gig. Following the instructions from the books he consulted, Jerry began training the dogs to be leaders. He would run with them in harness giving commands and demonstrating the meaning of each instruction: gee (go right), haw (go left), easy (slow down), pick it up (speed up).

Training was an exhilarating and rewarding experience. Jerry took great pride in watching the dogs respond to their training. The fact that they were so excited to run was very special. At the next club race, Jerry, Nikki and Princess entered the two-dog class and won.

Soon the LeVasseurs' backyard kennel began to grow and they acquired more dogs and had a few litters. With the Siberians, Jerry's goal was to maintain the running genes in the dogs.

Jerry's reputation in the sled dog circuit was also growing. After five years of winning races in the Southern New England circuit, it was time to race in the New England Sled Dog Club circuit.

Training now included proper nutrition, building strength before speed and having the young dogs learn from the veterans. Jerry had to be part vet, nutritionist, physical trainer and coach motivating the team. He introduced new dogs from renowned kennels and started earning victories in the big time circuit racing in New England, New York, Pennsylvania, New Jersey and Canada. To get to that level required experience, time and much effort. The results were very rewarding.]

The best team leader Jerry raised was Igloo Pac's Snow Bandit. Bandit was a champion whose sterling reputation preceded him in the dogsled circuit. A musher from Sweden once offered to buy Bandit for

$4,500. There was no way Jerry would sell such a special dog. Bandit was a trooper, who loved nothing better than racing. No matter what, Bandit wanted to run for Jerry.

Arden is also a dog lover. In addition to the sled dogs in the backyard kennel, she and Jerry adopted a couple of golden retrievers, first Tuck and then Robert. Arden dearly loved her goodhearted, golden pets. They spent their days in the backyard kennel, but also enjoyed family time inside.

In 2003, Jerry stepped back from sled dog racing. Slowly but surely, he found a new home for each member of his team. Jerry would miss the joy and satisfaction of training and running his dogs, as well as the relationships he had built with them, but it was time to move forward.

When Jerry and Arden retired in 2004, they sold their home in Madison and relocated to Brunswick, Maine. One member of the pack of racing dogs remained, Thunder. He moved with them to Maine.

After Thunder passed away, Jerry missed having a dog around the house. In order to enjoy some canine society, Jerry volunteered at the Midcoast Humane Society Adoption Center in Brunswick. He visited the animal shelter several times a week to help walk the dogs. One day, he met a handsome and friendly mixed breed named Buster. Each time Jerry went to the shelter, he looked forward to seeing his new friend. The two bonded and eventually Jerry brought Buster home with him. Once again, the LeVasseur household was complete.

Buster

Buster was a handsome and debonair fellow. He would affectionately lean against your legs and wait to be patted. He took great joy in playing with his toys, particularly a bright orange moose, and he danced around in circles at suppertime. Buster enjoyed going on invigorating runs with Jerry and loved to stretch out on the carpet in the sunroom in the evening keeping Arden company. Like all of the LeVasseur dogs, Buster was a beloved member of the family.

Jerry and his family have derived a lifetime of happiness by raising, caring for and training, playing with, and simply loving the many LeVasseur dogs who have come and gone through the years.

ठ ठ ठ

Snow, Serenity and Sleds

"There is nothing like going out from the starting line with a well trained team only hearing the panting of the dogs and the runners on snow." —Jerry

On February 5, 1978, as an unexpected blizzard with winds reaching 70 mph blew through the state, Connecticut was buried in more than two feet of snow. Businesses, schools and the roads were shut down for days. Slowly but surely residents of Madison and the other shoreline towns dug out from the storm.

On Princess Drive, Jerry LeVasseur and his family stayed warm by the fireplace and waited for the electricity to be restored. Outside in the backyard kennel, Nikki and Princess, along with four more Siberian huskies romped in the frozen drifts. Bred to thrive in snowy conditions, the dogs were in their element. Each night, the dogs joined the family by the fireplace to sleep. When the family ran out of groceries, Jerry hitched up the excited huskies and traveled by sled to a nearby store to stock up on supplies.

Two weeks later, Jerry and his team headed off to Cockaponset State Forest, the site of the Connecticut Valley Siberian Husky Club dogsled race. As Race Committee Chairman of the club, Jerry was thrilled with the perfect weather conditions. Two feet of snow covered the hilly terrain of the forest. The sun was shining and temperatures were predicted to rise to 30 degrees. The mushers and their dogs were in for a splendid day.

As the day progressed, children raced one dog teams and the adults ventured out onto the forest trails pulled by teams of up to eight dogs. Jerry ran his team of five. Led by Nikki, the huskies responded to Jerry's commands, working with him to run the best race possible. The bond between the dogs and their driver was unbreakable.

For his part, Jerry was enjoying the moment. Breathing in the crisp, cold air, taking in the sparkling white scenery and listening to the panting dogs and the scrape of the runners gliding over the snow.

Although Jerry was determined to put in his best efforts, more important than winning, was the thrill of being with his happy, well-trained dogs in such ideal sledding conditions. Snow is what the sport of dog sledding was all about and he was glad to be able to share the day with his team and the other mushers and their families who had gathered in the state forest.

Jerry continued to raise and race sled dogs for nearly thirty years. Because of the speeds and possible danger, it took courage to race a team. In Jerry's case, his hands added an extra hurdle to overcome. Extreme cold caused him pain and Jerry sometimes lost function in his hands by the end of the run, requiring help to unhitch and care for his dogs after the race.

Jerry and his team.

Despite these somewhat harrowing drawbacks, running his dogs was a challenge that was well worth enduring the cold, training in all types of weather and risking injury. Although he had some close calls—on one occasion he was nearly struck by a bullet fired by a hunter who was unaware of his presence in the state forest—Jerry remained a stalwart leader in the dog sledding community.

Jerry worked tirelessly on behalf of the Siberian Husky Club and his dogs. Highlights from his sledding and training career included many victories. Some of the accolades he and his dogs earned were first in the race, first in novice obedience, first in male sled dog show and top kennel. Jerry participated in the Siberian Specialty competition in Canada and had success at obedience trials in Bermuda. Jerry ultimately achieved the honor of being named a lifetime member of the New England Sled Dog Club.

Service has been an important part of Jerry's life. He is happy to serve and help others. As a member of various boards and a leader in organizations like the New England Sled Dog Club, Jerry has emphasized the importance of always keeping the true purpose of the group in mind. He represented his fellow mushers by communicating openly and with kindness, so they all could get the most out of each racing season.

In his exemplary career as a musher, Jerry had some mishaps and disappointments along with his successes. One unrealized goal was competing in the renowned International Sled Dog Championship held in the Adirondacks.

The invitation only race was held at Lake Placid. At the time, Jerry was known for having the best 6-dog team in New England. He often received calls from other mushers asking to use his dogs. Unbelievably, Jerry was not invited to participate in the championship. He could not understand why and worried that he was being excluded because the organizers feared he would not be able to maintain a solid grip on the sled. After the event, Jerry looked up the results and surmised that he and his team would have represented New England well.

Dogsledding is a family sport with character building responsibilities. The enthusiasm of the sled dog families and the dogs themselves at a race is something to behold. One of the most lasting rewards of participating in dogsledding was sharing his love of the sport with his family.

Arden accompanied Jerry to the races, on hand to help take care of the team. Suzanne accompanied Jerry to dog shows, working with their copper-colored Siberian, Penny. Karen and Kate both raced teams, earning medals and trophies like their dad. Karen then passed on her interest in dogsledding to her son, Justin.

Arden and Jerry's first grandchild, Justin was a curious and forthright little boy, who liked his grandparents' many dogs. When he was old enough, Justin began to accompany his Nan and Papa to the weekend dog races. In 1997, following in his mother's footsteps, the four-year-old competed in his first one-dog race in Laconia, New Hampshire.

At the starting line, Jerry hitched up Bandito. Justin climbed onto the runners, clutching tightly to the sled. Bandito was the son of Jerry's prized leader, Bandit.

Jerry and Karen, shouted, "Hold on!" as Bandito began to move along the course. Jerry was confident that Bandito, like his sire, would perform admirably for his young driver.

Justin and Bandito.

Justin held on, Bandito pulled with all his might, and they won the race. They were one-dog world champions. At the awards ceremony, Justin received a trophy that was practically bigger than he was. His dog sledding career was off to a promising start!

As for Jerry, his heart was filled with pride for his grandson, and joy for having the opportunity to provide him with such an exciting and memorable experience.

❡ ❡ ❡

Fitness, Fun and Friends

"Jerry is the best role model for hustle and helping others." — *Coach Peter Slovenski*

While rain drummed on the roof of the raised ranch on Princess Drive, Arden chopped carrots and cucumber to add to the wooden salad bowl on the counter. The comforting scent of tomato sauce filled the kitchen.

Jerry, methodically jogged up the stairs from the lower level of the house where his four daughters watched television, the aroma drawing him into the kitchen. Without pausing, he said, "That smells good. What's for dinner, Ard?"

"Spaghetti and meatballs," she called after him as he disappeared into the dining room.

He rounded the corner into the living room, jogged past the kitchen again and headed down the hallway toward the three bedrooms, where he turned around and jogged back to the stairway to make another circuit.

Normally, Jerry jogged outdoors through his neighborhood, but today the weather was uncooperative. Sticking to his fitness routine was important, so Jerry ran indoors instead.

A natural athlete, Jerry has focused on remaining fit and active throughout his life. As a child, he didn't want to feel sorry for himself or for others to pity him. Despite his injuries, he felt like he was just like everyone else and set out to prove that he could do anything he set his mind to doing.

At prep school, he played football and basketball. In college, he gave soccer a try, ran some track and joined the ski club. Most of his athletic endeavors involved playing inter-fraternity touch football and basketball for Sigma Phi. A dedicated competitor, Jerry was elected into the athletic organization, the Brown and White Society at Lehigh.

As he and Arden raised their children, Jerry incorporated his athletic pursuits into family life. During the summer, he played in a local softball league. His team was sponsored by Franco's Package Store, a local business that has been part of the Madison community for more than 5o years.

Jerry played in the outfield. Because of the injuries to his hands, he was unable to grasp the softball with his left hand to throw it. Undaunted, he developed a maneuver in which he dropped his glove and transferred the ball from hand to hand to throw it infield. He was so skilled at the maneuver that his fielding was not affected at all. At the plate, Jerry batted right-handed while guiding with his left hand.

On many summer evenings, Arden and the kids would join the other Franco's families at the field located near the town beach to cheer on the players. At the end of each season, everyone would gather together for a celebratory picnic, usually hosted by the captain of the team, Mr. White.

Strong bonds of friendship were forged among the players, as well as their wives and children. In the summer of 2o19, Jerry and Arden, attended a Franco's reunion in Connecticut. They reunited with old friends and reminisced about their days of glory on the softball field.

2019 Franco reunion in Connecticut.

Jerry and his family remained active during the winter months too. Many weekends, they made the drive up to Wilmington, VT, where they owned a ski chalet in a neighborhood called Chimney Hill. All four of the LeVasseur girls learned to ski at Haystack Mountain, a family friendly ski resort. In Vermont, the kids also enjoyed sledding and ice skating.

Kate tries out skiing at Haystack Mountain.

Skiing and dogsled racing were not the only winter sports Jerry attempted. He also took up snowshoe racing. In fact, at the age of 77, he placed fourth in his age group at a particularly grueling race held in Vermont near Chimney Hill. The course ran from the bottom of a ski area to the top. Despite having to make seemingly endless trips up and down portions of the mountain until he reached the bottom, Jerry persevered and finished the race.

Always up for a challenge, Jerry has been ready to try something new throughout his active life. From tennis and biking to snowshoeing and skijoring, he has run the gamut of athletic activities. His childhood difficulties made him stronger and fostered his competitive spirit. Jerry garners great satisfaction from setting goals for himself and not giving up until he has achieved them. He is thankful for being alive and wants to see and do as much as he can in life.

Skijoring race.

In his wide and varied travels, he has gone horseback riding in Bermuda, climbed the mast of a clipper ship on a Caribbean cruise and tried zip-lining in Costa Rica. Thankful for having overcome serious childhood obstacles and received so many blessings, Jerry does his best to live his life to the fullest.

Zip-lining in Costa Rica

Horseback riding in Bermuda.

Competitiveness, determination and a strong sense of fair play are also intrinsic elements of Jerry's character. Each of these qualities is embodied in the spirit of Olympism as defined by the founder of the modern Olympic Games.

In 1898, Pierre de Coubertins, wrote the first charter for the modern Olympic Games. Within the framework of the historic document, he defined his philosophy of Olympism. The French aristocrat dreamed of athletes from around the world competing against each other in a spirit of respect, friendship and inclusion. Additionally, each athlete would embody excellence and fairness. Jerry LeVasseur would have been an ideal candidate to participate in Pierre de Coubertins' modern games.

Although Jerry has never walked into an Olympic stadium as a competitor, on December 26, 2001, he had the opportunity to play a rewarding role in today's Olympic games. He was chosen to be one of the torchbearers as the Olympic flame was carried across the country from Atlanta to Salt Lake City in anticipation of the 2002 Winter Games.

The theme of the 2002 Olympic Torch Relay was inspiration. The torchbearers were selected from a pool of thousands of nominees. Arden nominated Jerry, sending the application directly to the Olympic Committee in Salt Lake City. The committee felt that Jerry met the four criteria they were seeking.

1. Jerry inspired others;
2. Jerry served his community in an exemplary manner;
3. Jerry embodied the Olympic spirit of achievement through sports and friendship; and
4. Jerry motivated others by overcoming adversity.

By December 26, 2001, the Olympic flame had reached New York City. Jerry had been selected to carry the torch for 2/10 of a mile that day as it made its way through Connecticut on its way to Providence, Rhode Island.

On the day after Christmas, Jerry proudly donned his official Olympic committee tracksuit and white knit hat worn by all of the torchbearers. He and Arden drove up to Hartford to take part in and bear witness to the historic Torch Relay. At his appointed moment, Jerry stood at his post, ready to receive the torch. After completing the hand-off, he set out, holding the torch aloft as he ran his portion of the relay course. Jerry and Arden then joined the crowds in Bushnell Park at the end of the route to celebrate the Olympic core values of excellence, respect and friendship.

Jerry's Olympic Torch Relay Plaque

Jerry treasures his memories of the Olympic Torch relay. He has devoted his life to sustaining the values that Pierre de Coubertins outlined in the Olympic Charter more than one hundred years ago. He values the friendships he has made with other athletes from around the world, he is always willing to lend a helping hand and he competes for the pure enjoyment taking on an athletic challenge.

At Bowdoin College, Jerry has passed on this Olympic legacy to the student athletes on the track and cross-country teams, inspiring them with his resounding motto, "fitness, fun and friends."

ǧ ǧ ǧ

From the Casual Jogger to Competitive Runner

"One of the thrills I get out of competing is when someone comes up to me afterward and says, 'you made me work hard.' That's more important than winning a medal." —Jerry

In 1977, Jim Fixx published his bestselling book, *The Complete Book of Running*. Fixx was a Mensa member, puzzle master and author of several puzzle books, who helped launch the 1970s physical fitness craze. He touted the physical and psychological benefits of regular exercise.

Upon reading the popular book on running, Jerry took Fixx's message to heart and took up jogging. He competed in his first road race at age 42. Sponsored by the Lion's Club, the 5-mile race took place in Jerry's hometown, Madison. He ran at a 7-minute pace. Although he did not place in the 40-49 age division, Jerry enjoyed the event and was satisfied with his performance. He believed that finishing the race was a triumph. He did not feel the need to place in the road race. His victories on the sled dog circuit fulfilled his competitive spirit at that time.

The joy Jerry finds in running is evident on the track and as he displays his medals and trophies won in Bermuda.

After the Lion Club race, Jerry kept competing. At one point, someone told him that as he continued training and competing his times would improve and they did. At the age of 48, Jerry ran his best times ever (17:07 in the 5K and 35:27 in the 10k).

Jerry has participated in competitive running for nearly four decades. He has racked up more than 1,000 first place finishes. He has competed locally, nationally and internationally. One of Jerry's favorite running destinations is Bermuda. He has competed at the Bermuda Marathon Weekend, running the 10K, the Half Marathon and the Bermuda Triangle Challenge several times. During each decade, he has continued to grow and develop as a competitor.

While setting and achieving new athletic goals throughout the years, Jerry has also gathered a plethora of happy memories. He recalls with pride competing against incomparable runners like George Jones and Ray Swan in the International Senior Games in Bermuda. When he was in his sixties, he was excited to attempt two new events: the steeplechase and the triple jump. He worked hard to perfect the skills needed to succeed in both events. Arden also competed in the triple jump event and Jerry coached her.

Jerry also enjoys the camaraderie of putting together and racing with relay teams. He and his team members have set records. Most recently, Jerry's team broke the United States and World Indoor Track records in the 4X800 relay for the over 70 and then the over 80 age group.

Every year, Jerry looks forward to competing in the Bad Ass Snowshoe Race (3, 4 and 5 miles) and Trail Run (6, 9 and 12 miles) series at Bradbury Mountain State Park in Pownal, Maine. He is usually the oldest competitor at the annual event. At one of the races, he had his picture taken with 9-year-old Ian Britt, the youngest entrant. Both Jerry and Ian are an inspiration to other runners.

Now that he has to walk over the roots and rocks to avoid falling, Jerry goes out early with the slower runners and then steps to the side on the course with his camera, so he can capture photos of the athletes as they run by. The reward for participating in the Bad Ass races (besides fitness, fun and friendship) is a winter hat with Bad Ass printed on it for doing all three snowshoe races and a Bad Ass hoodie for doing all three trail races.

Jerry proudly wears his Bad Ass gear from Bradbury Mountain.

Despite health issues, Jerry continues to run. He has overcome several bouts of cancer and trouble with blood clots in recent years, but has not let the illness or his treatments impede him. According to Peter Slovenski, Bowdoin track coach, Jerry "runs three times more races than college competitors do, and when you add up the distance of his races, he races four times the distance of our college runners."

A force to be reckoned with, Jerry first rose above physical adversity after suffering debilitating burns in the Hartford Circus Fire. Recently Dr. Herbert Paris, President and Chief Executive Officer of Midcoast Health Services, reviewed Jerry's childhood medical record and shared his reaction.

> "Jerry sustained a major injury in a historic circus fire. He suffered third degree burns over a major part of his body. Doctors did not give him much of a chance to live. The modern techniques of burn care were in their infancy in 1944, and antibiotic therapy had not yet been established.

His medical record traces and records his progress and painful recovery. His ability to tolerate many surgeries and long periods of rehabilitation is a tribute not only to his medical team but also to his personnel drive, his faith, his love of life and the power of positive thinking.

These traits have allowed him to enjoy a successful business career, an adoring family, exciting world travel, interesting hobbies and becoming a recognized world class runner Jerry has now taken his composite life experience and used it as a volunteer coach of the Bowdoin College women's cross-country and track teams. In addition to coaching the techniques of running, he inspires, motivates and encourages continuous improvement and a winning attitude" (Paris).

That winning attitude has sustained Jerry throughout his life, especially now. He has not let medical issues and related medications and procedures deter him. He consistently reminds himself of why he is competing in the first place: for fitness, fun and friendship.

As an octogenarian, Jerry run/walks a 16-minute mile and stays on soft surfaces like the golf course behind his neighborhood. He has slowed down, but he still sets goals for himself and has fun.

Although he may no longer be racing at the front of the pack, Jerry enjoys being out on the course walking or jogging with others and providing encouragement to his fellow competitors. As he did when racing his dogs, Jerry focuses on the pure enjoyment of the moment.

Jerry also continues to set goals for himself to maintain the fitness he has gained over the years. In the gym, he challenged himself to complete 7.6 to 8 miles in an hour on the lateral and zero runner machines. Recently, he broke his record on the lateral machine, running 4.58 miles in 33 minutes.

As an aging runner, Jerry does his best to train the whole body. His workouts include cross training, stretching, core, weight, balance, anaerobic and aerobic exercise. He makes full use of the Bowdoin fitness center and the indoor and outdoor tracks.

Jerry's impressive weekly training routine (described below in his own words) has allowed him to remain strong, fit, happy and healthy.

- At least 5 days a week I do the 17 weight bearing machines with 20 reps and core and stretching on a mat. The half hour also includes 20 squats on both sides of the Bosu half ball and 5 step-ups on a 28-inch box on both legs.
- I usually play tennis on Monday and Thursday for an hour and a half. I do the half hour workout before tennis.
- On Tuesday, I do 4.5 miles on the lateral elliptical out to ten at a level of 4 for 33 minutes. This includes doing a pace of 64-66 for a half lap and then increasing to 69-72 for the last half for an average pace of 67 or just over a 7:15 per mile pace. Next I do the half hour session as noted above finishing with 27 minutes on the zero runner doing at least 3 miles for between 7.5 and 8 total miles in an hour. The zero runner is a non-impact running machine.
- On Wednesday, I do the half hour session and an hour on the treadmill and elliptical combined. The treadmill is usually a fast walk with incline and maybe some running.
- On Friday I do the half hour, 20 minutes on the rowing machine, 30 minutes on an elliptical or treadmill, 5 minutes or 400 steps on the stair climber and 5 minutes on the curved non-motorized treadmill.
- Saturday and Sunday would be like Wednesday with variations unless I have a trail, snowshoe, track meet or road race.
- Depending on the weather, I do snowshoe running, cross country skiing, cycling, track training or running mostly on trails which may replace the daily sessions.
- During the week when I go to the Bowdoin track practice, I do the big warm up with the athletes.

Jerry truly believes that "the all body workout with intervals to raise the heart rate along with a good diet and positive attitude will help you enjoy life as you age and allow you to take on new challenges."

Maintaining fitness through sport and competition is a hallmark of Jerry's life experience. His athletic endeavors have had a positive effect on all areas of his life. Whether running at lunchtime to relieve stress at work, sharing his dogs' joy while racing through the quiet, snowy forest, or competing with Arden at Senior Games around the world, Jerry has reaped the benefits of staying active and fit.

෪ ෪ ෪

Jerry the Influencer

"Influencer (noun) : one who exerts influence : a person who inspires or guides the actions of others. " —*Merriam-Webster Dictionary*

An up and coming career for today's job-hunters is to become a social media influencer. Although Jerry cannot list this position on his professional résumé, he certainly qualifies as an influencer in the world of running. He has used his influence to inspire, advise and advocate for other athletes both as a coach and a fellow competitor. In numerous media interviews, he has shared his knowledge and philosophy of running.

One achievement that makes Jerry smile with gratitude and pride involves the Bermuda Marathon Weekend. While competing at age 77 along with two other runners, Jerry, who always looks to the future, wondered what they would do when they entered their eighties. There was no 80 and over age group. He spoke to the race organizer, Anthony, who took Jerry's suggestion of adding a new age bracket quite seriously. Three years later, Jerry and his fellow 80-year-olds were able to run the half marathon and 10K race in Bermuda.

One of Jerry's fellow athletes, Joe Cordero and his wife, have become great friends with Jerry and Arden. Joe and Jerry both compete in the steeplechase and they have put together record-setting relay teams. The two couples even enjoyed traveling together to Aukland, New Zealand for the World Masters Games.

Jerry's life story made such an impression on Joe that he was inspired to write a poem he titled "Heroes Among Us." Jerry was humbled when he

Heroes Among Us" by Joe Cordero

read the words Joe had written on a loose piece of paper. Wanting to preserve such an important keepsake, Jerry had the poem etched onto a wooden plaque.

Jerry has also been inspired to write on the topic of running (and travelling) himself. In the excerpted article below, Jerry offers glowing descriptions of his numerous trips to Bermuda where he competed in dog shows and ran in many road races. Perhaps, his words will influence other runners to make their own journey to the lovely island known for its pink sand and friendly population.

Running in Bermuda by Jerry LeVasseur

[Excerpted from an article published by the New England 65 plus Runners Club]

The first time my wife and I traveled to Bermuda was in 1964. We stayed at the Salt Kettle House Bed and Breakfast for $7 a night each. We loved the island and its people, some of the friendliest in the world. It was easy to get around by moped as long as you took care driving on the opposite side of the road and didn't panic. The food was very good and the scenery was fantastic.

We returned to Bermuda many times over the next 40 years staying at different hotels and resorts. On one trip when I was competing in obedience trials with two of my Siberian Huskies and attending the Connecticut CPA Society annual convention, we stayed in a suite at the Castle Harbor Hotel. We kept the dogs at a local kennel. The people at the kennel were great and we visited the dogs as much as possible, even taking them to play on the beach. Yukon and Cinder had just as much fun in Bermuda as Arden and I did.

We had promised our four daughters that we would take them to Bermuda when they graduated from college. Three years in a row, we traveled to Bermuda over Thanksgiving weekend with three other families, staying at the Reefs, one of our favorite resort hotels. We brought two daughters each of the first two years and then Arden's mother, Fran Crocker, the third year.

The Bermuda Marathon Weekend in January has always been one of my favorite events. I have attended the Marathon Weekend six times, staying at hotels like Grotto Bay and the Coral Reef. On our most recent visit, we reserved a room at the Fairmont Southampton, a superior property with a beach next to the famous Horseshoe Bay. The hotel had a fitness center, whirlpool and inside pool which I took advantage of. We also swam in the ocean. Luckily, the Marathon Weekend coincides with Bermuda's Restaurant Week. We have enjoyed affordable and delicious meals at the Mad Hatter, the Swizzle Inn and Waterlot.

On our most recent trips, we did not rent mopeds, which we felt would not be as safe as the bus. The bus system is very convenient and inexpensive. We saw a lot of the island riding around on the big pink buses and encountered the local residents in our travels.

Jerry running on Front Street in Hamilton

Bermuda is very hilly and can be windy and humid. Temperatures in January are usually in the 60s. Portions of the old railroad have been converted to public trails, so there are plenty of places to run in Bermuda. During my many visits, I would go jogging and often passed the legendary Johnny Barnes, a retired railroad worker who was known as Mr. Happy Man. Upon retirement, he would spend his mornings at the Foot of the Lane roundabout in Hamilton cheerfully greeting commuters on their way to work. Before his death at age 93, Bermuda erected a statue of Johnny at the roundabout. Over the years I had stopped to talk with him several times. The last time was five years ago when he was 91. He sat me down, holding both my hands and prayed. It was a moment I will never forget.

On one Marathon Weekend, I met a group from Jacksonville with blue shirts having a great time run walking. Their leader would say now run and after a few minutes he would instruct them to walk. After watching them run uphill and then walk down some hills, I told them that I was a volunteer coach at Bowdoin College and what they were doing would tire them faster. They took my advice and started calling me coach. I ran ahead of them but I could still hear them behind me. Part way up the hill at mile 5 I slowed and they caught up to me. As they passed, they urged me on saying, "Come on coach!" At the end of the race, we took a photo together. The next day I wished them well in the Half and they said they were ready since I had coached them well.

All of these experiences have provided memories I will always cherish. I highly recommend going to Bermuda, especially for the Marathon Weekend. The scenery, weather, volunteers and spectators make this a weekend not to miss.

ᛦ ᛦ ᛦ

Traveling the World with his Camera in Hand

"Once a year, go someplace you've never been before." — *Dalai Lama*

The LeVasseur family has taken the sage advice from the Dalai Lama to heart. When their daughters were young, Jerry and Arden often traveled abroad. They visited exotic destinations like Mexico, Scandinavia and the Caribbean. During each trip, Arden found gifts to bring home to the children. She selected souvenir country dolls from many of the destinations they visited, and the girls proudly displayed their doll collections on their bedroom bureaus. From Mexico, the girls received oversized, colorful sombreros and silver jewelry. These foreign souvenirs opened their hearts and minds to the wide world.

In the mid-1970s, the children accompanied Jerry and Arden on a family vacation to St. Maarten. They stayed on the Dutch side of the island near Little Bay. They enjoyed the beautiful weather, swimming and visiting the beach. Jerry also took everyone on a jeep tour of the island during which they encountered numerous goats. To top off the week, they took a day trip to the neighboring island of St. Barth. The LeVasseurs returned from their Caribbean sojourn happy, tanned and relaxed.

Family vacation to St. Maarten

Forty-something years have passed since that trip and Jerry and Arden have collected passport stamps from all over the world while traveling with her choir or to accounting conferences, to Senior Games competitions and for personal vacations. Arden has mailed postcards from all over the world to her family, sharing the beauty and wonder of their destinations in each hand-written message.

Jerry is also a fan of the postcard, but he prefers to document his travels with his camera, taking hundreds of photos at each destination he and Arden have frequented. Jerry has progressed from using film and a slide projector to take and share his photographs to becoming a master of the latest digital technology. He has taken photos of landscapes, architecture, wildlife, people and flowers all around the globe. Many of his images are as picturesque and compelling as any postcard. Viewers of his Flickr photostream can vicariously travel the globe through his myriad images.

Both Jerry and Arden value their world travels. They appreciate the opportunity to enrich their lives by exploring foreign lands, sampling unfamiliar cuisines, viewing natural wonders and talking with people from other cultures. Their travels have revealed that although we may seem different from one another, people all over the world simply want to enjoy life and be happy.

In September 2019, Jerry and Arden had the good fortune to travel to Alaska, where Jerry realized a lifelong dream. A long-time fan of the Iditarod Trail Sled Dog Race, Jerry always wanted to see the Iditarod Headquarters and some of the famous Alaskan kennels, including Happy Trails, owned by 4-time Iditarod winner, Martin Buser. He booked a room at Martin Buser's bed and breakfast where he and Arden toured the kennels. Jerry was particularly interested in examining Martin's sleds, trophies, trucks and trails, and of course, meeting the dogs.

A bit later in the trip, Jerry and Arden took a paddleboat river cruise to see the kennels of another 4-time Iditarod winner, Susan Butcher. Although Susan passed away from cancer, her husband, David, continues to maintain the kennels. Jerry enjoyed talking with both Martin Buser and David Butcher. Spending time at their kennels brought back many happy memories of his own dogsledding career.

Naturally, Jerry snapped many photos of the dogs and the kennels. He also had the opportunity to photograph moose, bears, foxes and eagles at Denali National Park, along with the stunning natural landscapes. This long-awaited trip, granted Jerry the chance to combine three of his passions: dogsledding, photography and world travel.

Photos from the September 2019 Alaska trip.

The LeVasseur daughters share their parents' inclusive worldview and passion for travel. Family conversations often revolve around memorable vacations. The sisters like to compare notes on favorite travel destinations and Arden and Jerry always have stories to share of their own global adventures.

Just a few months after the Alaska trip, Arden and Jerry, along with their daughters, sons-in-law and grandchildren, set sail on a cruise aboard the elegant Star Flyer clipper ship. The idea for this family vacation arose a year earlier at a holiday dinner. As they all sat around the dining table in Jerry and Arden's home in Brunswick finishing off the meal with one of Arden's decadent chocolate desserts, Jerry suggested the possibility of travelling together to the Caribbean.

The last time the family had all gone away together was back in 1999. Jerry and Arden were attending the Senior Games at Disney World, so the LeVasseur sisters had packed their suitcases and joined their parents in Florida.

Jerry, who is a wizard at finding travel deals online, followed up the 2018 holiday dinner discussion, by contacting a helpful travel agent, whose surname, ironically is Helper. The agent booked the Treasure Island clipper ship cruise for all the family members.

Prior to joining the cruise, Jerry and Arden spent two days in Philipsburg, St. Maarten. They stayed at a cozy and conveniently located hotel on the Back Street called Alicia's Inn. The family owned inn was named for Aunt Alicia, who inspired her loved ones with her entrepreneurial spirit.

During the two days in Philipsburg, they enjoyed exploring the shopping area and beach boardwalk of the colorful city. They swam in the ocean while listening to Christmas carols played along the boardwalk and sampled Caribbean cuisine at several local restaurants.

The highlight of their mini-vacation in St. Maarten was the island tour they took with a friendly and knowledgeable guide named John from Bernard's Tours. As they set off in his van, he warned that they might not be able to visit the French side of the island. The week before, there had been protests and the border had been closed.

The French side of the island.

The unrest was sparked by frustration over the slow recovery from the devastating effects of Hurricane Irma and dissatisfaction with the government's efforts to curtail rebuilding on waterfront property. As it happens, the roads were open once again and they crossed over to the French side. On the way to the capital city, Marigot, John pointed out burned cars and other signs of civil unrest. Hurricane damage was still evident on both sides of St. Maarten.

Touring the Dutch and French sides of the island with Bernard's Tours.

They capped off the tour back on the Dutch side with a stop at the Sunset Beach Bar at Maho Bay. The popular island destination affords a marvelous view of the planes taking off and landing at the nearby airport. Patrons can enjoy drinks and Caribbean cuisine at the bar, on the beach or lounging by the pool.

On Saturday evening, Jerry walked over to the St. Martin of Tours Catholic church with his second oldest daughter and youngest granddaughter to attend Mass before setting off on the Star Clipper cruise. The parish was so friendly and welcoming. At the end of the liturgy, the priest made announce-ments calling attention to a couple celebrating an anniversary and other special occasions of his parishioners. He also welcomed new visitors to the church. The spirit of inclusiveness made sharing Mass with the local residents a very special experience.

Saint Martin of Tours altar

The following day, the Star Clipper passengers began a week-long itinerary of beach hopping beginning with Sandy Ground on Anguilla. Travelling from the Star Flyer to the beach in the ship's tender on that first morning, Jerry and his family watched the distant beach come into focus. Brightly painted beach bars lined the shoreline and beach umbrellas sprouted from the sand like colorful flowers in a well-tended garden. Up above in the crystal clear cerulean sky, large seemingly prehistoric birds floated on the sea breeze. The LeVasseur clan happily settled onto the beach chairs lined up in front of Elvis' Beach Bar content to enjoy a day of reading in the sun, swimming, kayaking and walking the beach.

Of all the island beaches they visited—Jost van Dyke (where everyone feasted on beach barbecue and wandered down the shoreline to have a drink at the well-known Soggy Dollar), Norman Island (the "deserted" island they frequented on Christmas), and The Baths on British Virgin Gorda—the most memorable was The Baths.

The trip to the Baths National Park was an extra excursion offered by the cruise line. The adventurous passengers in the tour group (including Jerry and Arden) went on a rigorous hike to Devil's Bay. They made their way through the labyrinth of towering granite boulders scattered along the shore, walked through ancient caves and drank in the serene ocean views. Jerry, of course, took many stunning photos.

Virgin Gorda

Several members of the LeVasseur family took another memorable excursion on the island of St. Kitt's. One of the locals, graciously welcomed them into her home. A former teacher, she told them about the history of the island, its sugar cane industry and the rise of tourism. Now retired, she lives in a comfortable home overlooking the Atlantic beaches. From her balcony, she can also see St. Kitt's sister island, Nevis, on the horizon. The gracious hostess, served ginger beer and home-made Christmas cake, a special holiday treat. Everyone appreciated her warm and friendly hospitality.

The best thing about the week at sea for Jerry and Arden was having their children and grandchildren around them and creating family memories together. Throughout the week, everyone preserved those memories with their cameras. GoPros and iPhones. Jerry generously compiled all of the photos and videos on his Flickr page and created a comprehensive DVD slideshow, which he shared with everyone.

The memorable family vacation brought everyone closer together. The trip will remain a highlight in the LeVasseur family history. In coming years, Jerry and Arden, along with their daughters, will continue to heed the advice of the Dalai Lama and go somewhere they have never been at least once a year.

The LeVasseurs are a family of travellers.

ฆ ฆ ฆ

Fitness, Fun and Friends (Revisited)

"That's the story of Jerry's life..... running alongside others, and encouraging them that they can do it, and they can do better than they think they can." — *Peter Slovenski*

Throughout his long racing career, Jerry has gathered a circle of like-minded friends around him. At local and international road races, in the gym and on the Bowdoin campus, his gregarious and friendly nature has drawn people to him. Some of those friends have contributed amusing and inspiring "Jerry" stories, expressing their deep admiration and appreciation for the influence he has had on their lives.

Amusing tales by Bill Borla and Jerry LeVasseur

My friend, Jerry LeVasseur, has been the catalyst behind the trips to most of the track and field competitions I've gone to. If it were up to me, I never would have made it to any of them. Making travel arrangements wasn't my thing. Jerry was the travel agent, trip planner, tour guide and driver. How he had the stamina for it, I don't know. I guess he was just a bundle of energy. But I'm indebted to him because we have had a lot of fun times; and have seen some of the great natural and man-made wonders of the world.

In Connecticut, Jerry was known as Mr. Connecticut Senior Games. When he moved to Maine, he became Mr. Maine Senior Games. Besides the Senior Games and USATF national championships, Jerry got us into events like the Fifth Avenue Mile in Manhattan, the Lake Winnipesaukee Relay (8 person teams running 65 miles around the lake), the 200 mile Reach the Beach Relay in New Hampshire (12 person teams running 200 miles from the Bretton Woods Ski Resort to Hampton Beach in 24 hours), many cross-country team races and indoor relay races; and a 5 race pentathlon somewhere in Pennsylvania.

In our travels to Senior Games and USATF Championship events, Jerry and I have had some amusing experiences. Some of my favorite stories shared below exemplify Jerry's persistence, sense of fun and competitive spirit.

Dining out in Old San Juan—One year, we went down to Puerto Rico for the World Masters Athletics. The manager of the motel we were staying at recommended a restaurant in Old San Juan that he said was fantastic. So three of us drove there, looking forward to a good dinner.

On the doorstep of the restaurant, we were stopped by the maitre d'. She said we weren't properly dressed. We were wearing Bermuda shorts, but the dress code called for long pants. The motel manager hadn't said anything about a dress code and, anyway, we didn't pack any long pants.

We explained this to the woman, but she was dead set against letting us in, so we started to walk away. But Jerry is a very persistent fellow, and he convinced us to go back and try to change the mind of the maitre d'.

We turned around and approached her once again. We told her how the motel manager had recommended her restaurant, saying we shouldn't leave Puerto Rico without eating there. She asked us to wait a minute and went back inside. Soon, she came out with three very colorful, flowery tablecloths and told us to wrap them around ourselves and hide our Bermuda shorts.

Dining out in Puerto Rico
(photo courtesy of B. Borla)

We were in! We asked to be seated "in a dark corner." Unfortunately, the dark corner was in the back of the dining room and the place broke up laughing at three old guys wearing tablecloth skirts down to our ankles as we followed the maitre d' to our table. We would have fit right in at a Hawaiian luau. What we put up with to get a meal!

But that wasn't all. After finishing our delicious meal, we were trying to sneak out without drawing more attention to ourselves when Jerry tripped over his tablecloth skirt and knocked over a glass of wine on one of the tables. Of course, this drew all kinds of attention to us and we became the comedic relief on our exit!!

A Bellowing Moose—Another time we went to Pittsburgh for a Senior Games competition. We saw that there was an Arts & Crafts show going on and we went to look it over. We came upon a vendor selling Didgeridoos, which are 4-foot long, colorful tubes about 3 inches in diameter. You blow into one end and you're supposed to get a sound out the other end that sounds like the biggest, baddest bull moose bellowing during the rut.

The vendor needed a volunteer to try it and Jerry pushed me forward. The vendor showed me how to pucker up my lips and make the moose sound. I had visions of causing a stampede if there were any female moose around.

I took a deep breath and blew as hard as I could . . .

SQUEAK!!

I tried again . . . SQUEAK!!

"Are some of these supposed to sound like a mouse?" I asked.

No, only like a moose," the vendor replied. "Try again."

I blew even harder . . . SQUEAK!!

I was embarrassed because a lot of people had gathered around to watch and all I could do was SQUEAK!!
Finally, the vendor had enough and took away the Didgeridoo from me. I'm sure he was afraid I was going to ruin his chance of making any

sales. So I put my tail between my legs and walked away. That was as close as I came to making like a moose! Not very close at all.

Trainspotting — One time we were sleeping in a college dorm that I think was somewhere in Illinois. We were sound asleep when all of a sudden there was a horrific noise and the building started to shake. It sounded like a train was going to come right through the dorm.

Jerry and I jumped out of bed and we were so alarmed that we started running around in circles. When we finally settled down and looked out the window, we spotted a freight train on a track that was elevated on an embankment so that it was level with our room.

Those trains out in the Midwest are super long and the noise and shaking went on for some time. We figured the college had to pay the students to stay in that dorm.

The Importance of Hydration — For a marathon, or any race, proper hydration is a must. But before stepping up to the starting line, eliminating some of the liquid is also a must. Lines are long at a big race like the Montreal Marathon. What to do? When there is a crowd around a bush relieving themselves, you join them. After a short time, out comes a chipmunk looking bewildered about the storm of liquid.

Passing the Baton — At another competition, Jerry LeVasseur and Jerry Brown were running on the same 4x100 meter relay team. LeVasseur was supposed to hand the baton off to Brown. He came charging down the track to make the exchange. Apparently, Brown took off too slowly. LeVasseur barreled right into him, knocking him down.

From my seat in the stand, I roared with laughter because I thought it was one of the funniest things I'd ever seen on the track. Here are two guys on the same team dancing around with each other in the exchange zone, and the one who is supposed to be running is lying on the ground!

To top it all off, LeVasseur yelled at Brown to get up and start running. Brown protested that LeVasseur seemed more concerned about the race than he was about his well being. And that was true. Even if JB broke his leg, JL would have yelled at him to get up and get going.

Some people are just too competitive!

Battles of Winnipesaukee (Excerpt)— When I was in my 5os, some friends invited me to join their 8-man relay team that was going to run a relay race at Cape Cod. I declined because I thought it was too far to drive just to run one leg of the relay. Because of logistics problems at the Cape, the race was moved to a 66-mile course around Lake Winnipesaukee in New Hampshire and I gave in to my friends.

Despite my misgivings, I went, I ran and I absolutely loved it! It was so much fun to run with a group of great people, who were also great runners, instead of competing against them as an individual. The relay teams engaged in a friendly, but fierce, competition that played out over a number of years.

I often compared those runners to the sheriffs/gunslingers of the Old West—people like Wyatt Earp, Bill Hickock, Tom Mix, Red Ryder, The Lone Ranger, Buffalo, or Bill Cody. Some of those characters weren't real, but all the runners were and, although they weren't as notorious as the western variety, they were just as daring, adventuresome, courageous and resourceful.

Jerry, who was one of my teammates, would have thrived in the Old West. He is the super survivor. In 1944, when he was six years old, his mother took him to see the afternoon performance of the Ringling Bros. and Barnum & Bailey Circus in the north end of Hartford, CT. The big tent caught fire and over 160 people were killed, including Jerry's mother. Jerry's face and hands were badly burned and he lost parts of all his fingers. He doesn't know how he got out. The doctors thought he was going to die, but Jerry had other ideas. He survived because he is dogged in pursuit of the things he wants to do and doesn't let anything stop him. His story inspires me and our fellow runners.

The races around Winnipesaukee were awesome, exciting stories in themselves. Going back to my western analogy, you could say the races were a combination of a gold rush and the pony express. The races started at the Fun Spot at Weirs Beach with the runners on the first leg taking off en masse out of the parking lot, like the beginning of a gold rush. There are eight runners per team and the runners hand off a baton to a teammate at the exchange until all the legs are completed. It's like the pony express rider jumping off one horse and onto the next to continue delivering the mail until it reaches its destination.

In the 1993 race, our team, the Nifty Fifties set the course record running the 66 miles in 6:42:58 at a 6.108 minute pace. It was a tremendous battle that raged for the whole 66 miles among the Nifty Fifties, Greater Lowell, and the Class of 50-Maine. The team lineups and leg assignments were as follows:

	Dist.	Nifty Fifties	Greater Lowell	Class of 50-Maine
1	10.7	Pete Madden	Colin Gouldson	John Noyes
2	11.0	Bob Seiller	Doug MacGregor	Bob Coughlin
3	10.5	Danny Klein	Jack Pierce	Bob Payne
4	4.0	Jerry LeVasseur	George Bisson	Joe Richards
5	10.8	Bob Graham	Charlie Pratt	Myles Lemeu
6	6.4	Bill Borla	Bob Ludwig	Bob Gillespie
7	8.5	Nick Collin	Denny LeBlanc	Bruce Bell
8	4.4	Hal Bennett	Will Mason	Doug Ludwig

My advice to any runner is, if you get invited to join a relay team, give it a try. You might just love it. And I'm sure Jerry would agree.

Bill Borla
Torrington, CT

Camaraderie at the Gym

I retired to Brunswick, Maine several years ago and early on met Jerry LeVasseur at Bowdoin's Buck Fitness Center. During one of my daily workouts, I noticed this other oldster doing more exercise than I. We introduced ourselves and talked for a while.

In short order, I learned about his early life and the tragic event in Hartford. Being about six months older than Jerry, I remembered the circus fire. I also found out that he was a volunteer Bowdoin track coach.

And then, not so slowly but surely, I learned about Jerry's other unique attributes and accomplishments.

First and foremost, I learned that at his age he was an active and, more often than not, winning competitive runner in the 'senior circuit'. The circuit encompassed not only Brunswick and its environs, but all over the US and abroad!

I discovered that he was an active and regular squash and tennis player, sports I had given up long ago.

As I got to know him, Jerry regularly bested me and most of the other Buck regulars in doing thousands of steps on the stair climber. And he and I compete almost daily for the one exercise wheel (so far it hasn't come to fisticuffs).

The fact is that Jerry and I are two very lucky people! We've both had surgical interventions too numerous to discuss here and we're both still active and here to tell the tale! And, what is more, neither of us has any plans to stop what we've been doing!

Dick Burns
Brunswick, ME

A Volunteer Extraordinaire

Jerry has been like a combination of a coach, a professor, and a pastor to our runners. As a coach he helps the team with his knowledge of training and racing. As a professor, he helps the team with stories about running history and American history. As a pastor he helps the team with inspiration, and advice on facing and overcoming adversity.

Jerry has a great message to the team about running through the line, and not slowing down just before the line. He teaches students to never give up. He is the best role model for hustle and helping others. When there is an assignment at a track meet such as setting out cones, or handing out umpire flags, Jerry hustles to get the job done. He is exceptionally adept at timing races.

Our timers are expected to time one group of runners at a time. Timing two groups usually leads to a timer error such as missing the times of one group of runners. With all the different workout distances and paces, it's just too hard to time more than one group on a 200-meter track.

The runners come by roughly every 30 or 35 seconds. I can do it because I have a lot of experience, I'm still young enough, and I'm a professional timer. Jerry followed the one group timing rule for one year, and watched me time two groups. Sure enough, by his second year he was timing two groups at once, and hustling back and forth to the different lines yelling out splits to multiple groups as though he was a professional coach. And by his third year, he would even enjoy showing us all up by timing THREE groups at once.

That's the story of Jerry's life—one activity, one endeavor, one mile, and one minute at a time, doing better than others thought he would do.

Members of the Bowdoin track team practice the steeple chase.

Most significantly, Jerry has an incredible gift for reaching out to help so many people. While racing, he encourages other runners and gives them advice. Jerry knows how to be a tough competitor, but in some races he has time to find out the Personal Record times, and goals of other runners. Then he talks to them about things he has learned that can help them do better than they thought they could.

That's the story of Jerry's life—running alongside others, and encouraging them that they can do it, and they can do better than they think they can.

We owe Jerry many thanks for running alongside the Bowdoin track program and helping us do better than we thought we could.

Coach Peter Slovenski
Bowdoin College
Brunswick, ME

Giving Back at Bowdoin College

"Jerry has been like a combination of a coach, a professor, and a pastor to our runners."
— *Coach Peter Slovenski*

The cross-country athletes ran in a ragged line, their sneakers pounding against the dusty dirt road leading steeply uphill. Brisk gusts of wind swept down the road sending fallen leaves dancing in the air. Above them, the water tower stood resolutely silhouetted against the mostly overcast autumn sky.

Although their calves burned with fatigue and their hearts pounded in overdrive, the runners kept up the pace. Coach Jerry, as was his tradition, had promised to reward the team with a trip to the local gelato shop at the end of practice.

Jerry ran alongside the college students, shouting words of encouragement as he passed them. The team watched him in amazement and then pushed on, determined to keep up with their eighty-year-old coach.

When he and Arden moved to Brunswick, Maine in 2004, Jerry offered his services as a volunteer for the track team at Bowdoin College. He wanted to give back to the sport that had been so good to him. Soon the scene described above would become an annual, much anticipated event in Jerry's life.

Despite the coach, Peter Slovenski's wariness of taking on volunteers, he decided to give Jerry a chance. Jerry began volunteering with the Cross Country team. He worked tirelessly with the young athletes helping with anything the coach needed from timing runners and measuring courses to painting hurdles and taking photographs. After just two practices, the coach was sold. His new volunteer knew how to hustle and embraced a strong work ethic.

Slowly but surely, Jerry expanded his duties and responsibilities at practices and meets. He coached the student-athletes who wanted to compete in the steeplechase events and was also promoted to take on the role of Head Coach for the JV team. He perfected his skills as a timer and shared his thousands of meet photographs with parents who were unable to be there in person and the athletes themselves who wanted to study their form and technique.

With pride and satisfaction, Jerry has noted, "I love what I do and the satisfaction from helping others is amazing."

For all of his hard work and dedication, Jerry has received the Polar Bear Award and joined the ranks of inductees into the Volunteer Officials Hall of Fame.

In 2011, the coach requested that Jerry attend the annual awards ceremony because two members of the track team were to be honored. Christina Argueta '11 received the Academic Achievement Award For Women, an award that honors "a senior varsity female student-athlete with the highest grade-point-average combined with accomplishments in athletics over the past seven semesters" (Bowdoin). Molly Duffy, also a senior was awarded the Anne L.E. Dane Trophy, which honors the memory of the wife of Francis S. Dane, Class of 1896. It is awarded to "the senior member of a women's varsity team who best exemplifies the highest qualities of character, courage and commitment to team play" (Bowdoin). Of course, Jerry wanted to be there to cheer on his athletes.

The emcee kicked off the ceremony by announcing the winner of a special award given to someone outside the Bowdoin community who has demonstrated outstanding support of Bowdoin athletics. Sitting in the back of the theater beside Arden, Jerry was incredulous when his name was called. Wondering what he was supposed to do, Jerry exchanged a glance with his wife. He stood at his seat and waved to acknowledge the honor, but was called up to the stage. He received a handsome clock and said a few words of thanks. The student athletes were glad for the opportunity to cheer on their hardworking coach.

Jerry and his student athletes at award ceremony

Jerry has shared not only his victories with the student athletes, but also difficulties and disappointments. On two occasions, he was unable to complete a race due to fatigue and being overheated. He is not proud to have walked off the track, feeling he let down his team. These incidents illustrate the importance of being aware and listening to your body. Although Jerry teaches the students to "run through the finish," he also wisely counsels them to take care of themselves and avoid injury.

Impressed with all the student athletes handle during the school year from academics to athletics and adjusting to campus life, Jerry is compelled to offer them his support and guidance. He has stated on more than one occasion that their successes are more fulfilling to him than his own accomplishments.

Eternally grateful for Coach Jerry's advice, encouragement and camaraderie, several of the Bowdoin athletes, along with his fellow coaches, have shared stories of their best memories of working with him.

A beloved tradition and a new challenge

Coach Jerry has been a huge influence on both the cross-country and track and field teams at Bowdoin. I first met him when I joined the cross-country team during my freshman year. Coach Jerry always leads the JV workouts and he makes practice fun. Whenever we perform mile repeats on the Bowdoin cross-country course, Coach Jerry greets the runners with a big smile as he waits with the stopwatch at the end of the run.

He doesn't always stay on the sidelines. When he schedules a dreaded Water Tower Hill workout, Coach Jerry runs alongside the team and cheers us on. At the end of the season, we always do one last run to the top of Water Tower Hill and then Coach Jerry takes us to Gelato Fiasco to celebrate. The people at the gelato shop should definitely name one of their flavors after Coach Jerry.

On the track team, I decided to give the steeplechase a try, and Coach Jerry was a big help. He has a lot of experience in the event and actually still competes in steeplechase races. He taught me some conditioning stretches and showed me how he now steps over a hurdle. When I started out on the steeple course, I used his stepping over technique until I was confident enough to leap over the hurdles. There's no doubt in my mind that Jerry would still jump over the hurdles too if he could. Coach Jerry also advised me on the best way to handle the water jump.

The steeplechase is a fun, rewarding and difficult event. My teammates and I have formed a special bond with each other and with Coach Jerry. We admire him for his dedication and good sportsmanship. He shares his joy of the sport and his own running experiences with us all. I feel honored to work with someone who has been such an inspiration to so many athletes. Because of Coach Jerry, running and keeping fit will always be part of my life.

Holly Lyne
Bowdoin College
Class of 2021

Jerry and his team at Gelato Fiasco

Finding joy and daily gratitude

Every few years, Coach Jerry shares his story about the Hartford Circus Fire in front of the whole team. His story continues to resonate with the students and provides perspective on the importance of finding joy, and finding daily gratitude in life.

A true role model for the team, Coach Jerry has always preached fun, fitness, and friends to our student-athletes. I can recall multiple times when the students have quoted those words back to me. I, myself have quoted him. His positive philosophy keeps me motivated to stay active and truly love what I do as a coach!

Lara-Jane Que
Assistant Coach
Bowdoin College

An Inspiration for a Life Well Lived

I was lucky enough to have Jerry as a coach throughout my time running cross-country and track and field at Bowdoin College. Jerry dedicated countless hours and patience as my steeplechase mentor. He taught me the proper drills, form and technique, and strategies to master hurdles and the nuances of the discipline.

While I appreciated Jerry's tutelage and running expertise, I admired him more for the thoughtfulness and care he put into his relationships with student athletes. When I studied abroad in New Zealand, Jerry let me borrow videos, maps, and notes from his trips there. During the doldrums of winter running, Jerry lent me racing snowshoes to venture out into the icy trails of Commons. Last, I will always remember having a senior pot-luck dinner at Jerry's house—we played yard games, ate fried chicken, and tried on his assortment of exotic hats.

Jerry was more than a coach; he was a defining part of the team culture. Jerry set the stage for many of my favorite memories and moments from running at Bowdoin.

Funnily enough, it was upon graduating that I truly realized the importance of Jerry in my Bowdoin experience. After my senior year, I worked in the Sustainability Office. As part of my weekly routine, I would lift weights or workout at the Buck Fitness Center on Monday and Wednesday mornings. It so happened that was the exact same time Jerry and his gang of white haired retirees would also exercise. Waving at Jerry across the jungle of weight machines, chatting about the cross country team's latest results, or getting filled in on the latest race that Jerry had completed, was an integral part of my gym experience.

Whenever Jerry was jet-setting across the country or globe to smash some senior national or world record, the gym was quiet and lifeless in his absence. Jerry was more than a coach, he was an essential presence in my life at Bowdoin. A positive smile, a helping hand, a training partner, and an inspiration for a life well lived.

Bridger Tomlin
Bowdoin College
Class of 2017

Conquering Water Tower Hill

Water Tower Hill is not a source of many happy memories. The climb from the base of the hill to the water tower overlooking Brunswick was short but painfully steep, and by the twelfth repeat, legs turned to lead. The workout at Water Tower Hill was a staple of the Bowdoin junior varsity cross country team, and one that most who experienced it would like to forget.

But one happy memory persists. It was freshman year, and Coach Jerry selected me and another classmate to lead the final four repeats. We labored up the hill in double file, a dozen exhausted runners in tow. As we reached the halfway point of the climb, I heard footsteps coming up alongside me on my right. Somewhat peeved, I assumed a runner had broken rank to push the pace. But there was Coach Jerry, a septuagenarian, darting past us up the hill as if to say, "See, it's not so hard!" It was just the inspiration we needed.

Bowdoin runners make their way up Water Tower Hill

Over the years, Coach Jerry has provided a constant source of inspiration to scores of Bowdoin runners. His life is one of overcoming adversity and breaking through barriers to achieve his maximum potential--all while maintaining a positive outlook and a great sense of humor. This has made his work with the junior varsity team particularly impactful. He served as a daily reminder that any runner could improve, regardless of the challenges they faced, if they resolved to work hard, dedicate themselves, and keep the right attitude.

Thanks to Coach Jerry's guidance and training, I, like many other junior varsity runners, made the transition to the varsity squad. So it was particularly meaningful to have Coach Jerry cheering at my final cross-country race at Williams College, a race that was the culmination of so many long miles and difficult workouts.

After the race, as I drove the team van back home through the hills of Western Massachusetts with Coach Jerry seated next to me, I couldn't help but think back to Water Tower Hill, for there was Coach Jerry alongside me once more, with a dozen exhausted runners in tow.

I will always remember Coach Jerry when I think back to Water Tower Hill, and for me, that makes it a truly happy memory.

Charlie Berdahl
Bowdoin College
Class of 2011

Balancing competition and fun

I have many fond memories of Jerry as a truly kind and warm-hearted person. What I remember most about Jerry as a coach is that he always stressed, in his unassuming way, that running should be a balance between competition and fun.

While Jerry never ceased to give insightful advice on technique, he also always tried to inspire us to appreciate the moment and to enjoy ourselves. I can't tell you how many times in the middle of a punishing steeplechase race, I would look up and see Jerry with a smile on his face. Without fail, it would give me a little extra boost — especially because I knew as soon as I got within earshot, I'd hear him saying, "you have to pick it up!"

Ben Torda
Bowdoin College
Class of 2018

Coach Jerry's inspiring words still resonate

Coach Jerry comes to mind often. Phrases from the speeches he delivered to us before meets replay in my head. I particularly remember that during pre-season my senior year, he gave a presentation about the Hartford Circus Fire, in which he lost his mother. I expected him to exhibit some anger about what many consider to have been a preventable tragedy. Instead, he applied the lessons he learned from it to us and our training. I was stunned! How could he compare something so serious to something as elemental as running a race?

There's a Barbara Sher quote that says, "It's essential to distinguish between events that are really beyond your control and events you caused yourself." I appreciate these words because the meaning behind them is that a person should own up to his or her own mistakes rather than pity oneself and blame outside forces, especially when there are a number of events in life that are truly out of our control.

Many of the hardships that Jerry has gone through (cancer, the loss of his closest loved ones, among others) have been entirely out of his control. Thus, according to this quote, he could feel sorry for himself. He could ask "why me?" and feel justifiably frustrated with his circumstances. But in the time that I've known him, Jerry has never once pitied himself.

As he demonstrated in this presentation, he takes the most valuable lessons from the unimaginable challenges he's faced and shares them with us. He's focused on things he can control (heck, he can keep racing!!). Whenever Jerry shared advice with us as a team about how we should control what we can in our competitions and ignore that which we can't, I took it far more to heart than when he said it because he lives by this philosophy.

His words continue to pop back into my head when I face minor adversities and his words empower me to carry on.

Julia O'Rourke
Bowdoin College
Class of 2019

Overcoming adversity

Soon after Jerry started as a volunteer coach with the Bowdoin track program, I asked him if he would be willing to do a presentation on the 1944 Hartford Circus Fire. For students on a college track team, I thought it would be a powerful educational event that included history, medicine, philosophy, and family. Jerry agreed to do a presentation, but he said he would only do it once every four years so each student would just hear the presentation once during college.

Jerry started out with some background about World War II America, and the way he and his mother approached the circus that day. Then he switched over to a 40 minute History Channel documentary movie about the Fire.

After the movie, Jerry gave some more details about what he remembers from the Fire. Our students sit through a lot of presentations during a school year and a track season, but the atmosphere in the room was filled with attention and quiet as Jerry described the way his mother protected him as they fell to the ground. The students remained intensely attentive as Jerry went on to talk about adversity.

"I faced a lot of teasing in the school yard for what the fire had done to my upper body," he said. "Kids can be cruel to each other, but I didn't let that stop me from trying anything I wanted. People saying you can't do something can motivate you.

He shared one of his memories from the day of the fire. When he was lying in a state of semi-consciousness in the hospital after the fire, he overheard the doctors saying they didn't think he was going to make it.

Jerry said to himself, "Oh yes I am going to make it."

He went on to explain that you can let adversity stop you, or you can decide that you are going to do something in spite of adversity. And you can make a habit of doing your best through adversity time after time so instead of letting adversity give you an excuse about why you couldn't do something, adversity becomes a motivation to do better because of it.

He concluded the story by saying, "You run into adversity throughout life, and I guess I was lucky that I ran into it early because it taught me for the rest of my life to try harder when I encountered adversity."

Jerry talked for several minutes about the competitive endeavors of his life such as dog sled racing and road racing. He described the challenges of what he does, but he spent more time talking about the rewards of the discipline of dog training and the camaraderie of running.

He then spent some time talking to the students about the life-long benefits of running after college. In a presentation about an incredible tragedy, he spent most of his time talking about running lessons, and the positive perspective he has learned from his experiences.

When he finished his 60-minute presentation of talking, watching the movie, and talking some more, he got a standing ovation from the 80 students in attendance.

Peter Slovenski
Track and Field Coach
Bowdoin College

⚇ ⚇ ⚇

Afterword

"Thus dwelt together in love these simple Acadian farmers,
Dwelt in the love of God and of man." — Henry Wadsworth Longfellow, **Evangeline**

The LeVasseur family can trace its roots back to the French settlers in southeastern Quebec and the New Brunswick Acadians. The Acadians immigrated to North America from Île-de-France, Normandy, Brittany, Poitou, and Aquitaine.

In the mid-eighteenth century, the British forced them from their farms and their fishing villages. When the war between Britain and France ended, some of the displaced Acadians returned to their homeland, but still faced prejudice and oppression from the Anglo majority. The resilient French Canadians endured, forming close-knit communities centered around the Catholic church and remaining steadfast in their desire to preserve their Acadian culture (Ancestry).

The Acadian strength and spirit of adventure live on in Jerry LeVasseur. Like his Violette and Cyr ancestors, Jerry has confronted and overcome adversity. Thankful that God helped him survive the fire, recover from his injuries and go on to build a happy and eventful life, Jerry continually looks to the future, to what comes next.

Following his advice to the Bowdoin athletes, he plans to run through the finish line Most assuredly, Jerry will take on whatever comes next in his life with his characteristic optimism, faith, and determination.

ŏ ŏ ŏ

Lifetime Achievements

- Jaycees Connecticut Outstanding 10 Year award
- Lifetime membership in the International Jaycees
- Spark Plug and Jaycee of Month Awards
- United States Jaycee Spoke Award
- Jaycee Presidential Award of Honor Chairperson of Projects recognition
- Member of Board and Treasurer

- President, Treasurer of Local and International clubs
- 6 Six Dog, 3 Eight Dog, 2 Four Dog and 3 One Dog { Justin} Club Championships
- NESDC Best Overall Kennel Award,
- Sportsmanship Award
- Several Outstanding Dog Race and Obedience Awards
- High Scoring Obedience Dog in Bermuda
- Outstanding Lead Dog Award
- Several Superior Sled Dog
- Best Team Awards Recognition by The Siberian Club of America for service on Race Committee
- Professional life Chairman of CSCPA

- Annual Meeting Committee CFO with Company (37 Years in Corporate Financial Dept)

- Over 1,000 1st places in age groups including several overall 1st places in races
- Individual National Championships in Steeplechase, Indoor Triple Jump, 8K Cross Country and Track 10K.
- Many All American Standards met in Track and Field
- Over 75 National Relay and Team National and Region Championships including 7 National Relay Records Numerous Road Race Records
- 2 World Relay Records
- 3 World Relay Marks

- 8 World Master Games Medals including 1 Gold 7 Bermuda International Senior Games Medals (5 Gold and 2 Silver)
- Numerous Senior International Medals and Ribbons.
- 5 Maine records set. Corporate Track records set: 9 at 70-79 and 10 at 80-89
- Inducted in the Maine Running Hall of Fame, the Maine Senior Games Hall of Fame, the New England 65 Plus Runners Club Hall of Fame and the Bowdoin Volunteer Officials Hall of Fame
- Presented the Maine Track Club Lifetime Achievement Award
- Best in Age Group Awards
- Winner of the 80+ Division of the Grand Prix
- Come Back Runner of the year
- Special Achievement Award
- Presented the Martin's Point Health Care Medallion Award for work with Maine Senior Games in promoting Health and Fitness Recognition
- Plaque for 7 years of service on the National Senior Games Association Board
- Recognition plaque for service as President on the New England 65 Plus Runners Club
- Received the Polar Bear Award for Outstanding Support of Bowdoin Athletics
- Ran in the 2002 Salt Lake Winter Olympics Torch Relay
- Received the Personal Best Award from the National Senior Games Association
- Named one of 30 who helped National Senior Games reach its 30th Anniversary
- Twice received the Maine Corporate Track Association
- Tim Smith Award for outstanding distance running
- Triple Crown and Grand Prix Winner
- Eight Marathons Finished including Boston
- Maine USATF age group champion in cross country and several indoor and outdoor track events
- New England USATF age group champion in several indoor and outdoor track events
- Nominated for Rev. Joe Shea Award
- A beloved wife and 4 fabulous daughters

To achieve goals and overcome adversity one needs help, support and encouragement along with a positive attitude, determination, hard work and the ability to address the issue head on. Jerry is thankful for the support, friendship, encouragement and loyalty of so many people who have helped him along the way to achieve his goals and shared in his achievements.

In sled dog racing, family and competing friends like Bruce Crowther and Dr. Rob Tucker made it fun and rewarding. As mentors and friends, Jerry learned much from the top sled dog drivers like Dr. Charley Belford, Dr. Roland Lombard, Terri Killam and Harris Dunlap. Jerry purchased his best dogs and leaders from the last three.

In athletics (running and track events), friends like Bill Borla, Joe Cordero, Bill Spencer, Bill Riley, Bob Randall, Harry Carter, Zeke Zucker, Tom Butterfield, John Dugdale, Geof Etherington and Phil Pierce, to name a few, lent their support to Jerry by running on his teams.

Older runners who were an inspiration are Joe Ferandez, Lou Peters, Mary Haines and Polly Kenniston, all members of the New England 65 Plus Runners Club Hall of Fame. Bob Payne and Scott Brown, members of the Maine Running Hall of Fame, have supported and inspired Jerry in his running.

What keeps Jerry feeling young and still moving is the determination and hard effort of the Bowdoin athletes.

Ian Parlin and Ryan Triffitt, founders of the Trail Monsters trail and snowshoe race series, taught Jerry that being competitive is okay but it is better to be a badass running in the woods over roots and rocks enjoying nature.

Jerry has benefitted as a member of several running clubs including the New England 65 Plus Runners Club, Mohegan Striders, Moose Milers Running Club and Wolfpit Running Club.

After moving to Maine, Jerry started running with the ATP (Aged to Perfection) group on the weekend when not racing. It is a fun group made up of some excellent athletes who have stopped competing.

Jerry believes in cross training and one sport that does that is tennis. The 80 plus group that gets together every Monday and Thursday for an hour and a half to have fun and get some exercise are Al Fuchs, Hody White, Skip Bartlet, Ray Fisher and now deceased Charley Butt and Harry Warren. All good athletes who are fun to compete with.

What has been most fun for Jerry is travelling with Arden to National Senior and World Masters Games where both compete and upon finishing competition for the day go off to see the sights. Arden has competed mostly in swimming events but now does the long and triple jump with Jerry's coaching. Jerry is proud to note that Arden has now earned more gold medals than he has.

Senior Games both local and national have been special for both Arden and Jerry offering an enjoyable path to fitness through sport. The games are a good example of fitness, fun and friendship. They have made friends all over the world through sport. Both Jerry and Arden want to compete as long as they can with the next age group being 85.

🎖 🎖 🎖

Additional Reading

Altimari, Dave, et al. "The living survivors of the Hartford circus fire still carry the scars from the tragic day. Hear their stories in this interactive oral history," *The Hartford Courant*, 27 Jun 2019, www.courant.com/news/ connecticut/hc-news-living-survivors-of- the-hartford-circus-fire-20190627-vrr7uu2qibdljky5da3qo66yr4-story.html.

"Athletic Department Awards," *Bowdoin College*, 20 May 2020, athletics.bowdoin.edu/sports/2020/5/20/information-history-awards.aspx.

"Canadian Maritimes Acadians." *Ancestry*, 2020, ancestry.com/dna/ origins/4475B3D2-B5C9- 4DB9-B8E487589EF821CF/details ?branch=FRAM2019_4.1&time=1900.

"Forever Run Newsletter." *New England 65 plus Runners Club*, 2020, www.ne65plus.org/index.php ?page=newsletter.

Goode, Steven. "His mother died saving his life during the Hartford Circus Fire, but Jerry LeVasseur turned a catastrophe into a lifetime of opportunity.' *The Hartford Courant*, 6 July 2019, www.courant.com/community/hartford/hc-news-hartford-circus-fire-jerry- levasseur-20190706-rqnk2ymhmffgne 4bngmj63fp7i-story.html.

Grammer, Geoff. "National Senior Games: Fire Survivor has Enjoyed a Lifetime of Defying the Odds." *Albuquerque Journal*, 22 Jun. 2019, www.abqjournal.com/1331926/defying-the-odds- 2.html? fbclid=IwAR1cSn8sfSBJxXCUCrmyWZazIjzwgqekG5RT7kpEgFE8IrrbvYZ ORlx5xRQ.

Longfellow, Henry Wadsworth. "Evangeline." *Evangeline & Selected Tales and Poems*, Signet Classics, 2005.

Moon, Del. "The Show Must Go On." *2014 Personal Best*, May 2014. *National Senior Games Association*, NSGA, 2020, nsga.com/the-show-must-go-on/.

Neil, Scott. "Indomitable Spirit of Late Starter Inspires." *The Royal Gazette,* 17 Jan. 2019. www.royalgazette.com/runningtriathlon/article/20190117/indomitable-spirit-of-late-starter-inspires.

O'Nan, Stewart. *The Circus Fire: a true story of an American tragedy.* Random House, 2008.

Skidgell, Mike. *The Hartford Circus Fire ~ July 6, 1944.* 7 July 2020, www.circusfire1944.com.

Swatek, Randall. "From the Yukon to Cockaponset, It's a Dog's Life." *New York Times*, 19 Feb. 1978. p. 21.

Treadwell, David, "Unsung Hero: Jerry LeVasseur of Brunswick, steeled by fire." *Portland Press Herald,* 6 Aug. 2015, www.pressherald.com/2012/07/09/unsung- hero-jerry-levasseur-of- brunswick-steeled-by-fire/.

About the Author

Linda A. LeVasseur is the author of two novels, *Forget-Me-Not* and *Sandra Cahill's Best Friend*. She writes contemporary fiction for women and young adults.

She lives outside Boston with her husband and their dog and cat. Like her father, she enjoys biking, traveling and taking photographs.